GIRL TALK

How to survive

ZITS AND BAD HAIR DAYS

Lisa Miles and Xanna Eve Chown

rosen publishing's
rosen central

NEW YORK

This edition published in 2014 by:

The Rosen Publishing Group, Inc.
29 East 21st Street, New York, NY 10010

Designer: Jeni Child
Editor: Joe Harris
Consultants: Gill Lynas and Emma Hughes
Picture research: Lisa Miles and Xanna Eve Chown
With thanks to Erin Darcel
Picture credits: All images: Shutterstock

Library of Congress Cataloging-in-Publication Data

Miles, Lisa
How to survive zits and bad hair days/[Lisa Miles and Xanna Eve Chown].—1st ed.—
New York: Rosen, c2014
        p. cm.—(Girl talk)
Includes index.
ISBN: 978-1-4777-0709-8 (Library Binding)
ISBN: 978-1-4777-0724-1 (Paperback)
ISBN:978-1-4777-0725-8 (6-pack)
1. Girls—Growth—Juvenile literature. 2. Girls—Physiology—Juvenile literature.
3. Puberty—Juvenile literature. 4. Adolescent embarrassment—Juvenile literature.
I. Chown, Xanna Eve. II. Title.
RJ144 .M55 2014
612.6'61'08352

Manufactured in China

CPSIA Compliance Information: Batch #S13YA: For further information, contact Rosen Publishing, New York, New York, at 1-800-237-9932.

Contents

LIFE IS A roller coaster!

One day you feel like a little kid, and the next morning you wake up and suddenly – bam! You're a teenager. It's time to stop playing and start dealing with real life: periods, bras, bad skin and mood swings. Right?

Well, sort of! Puberty is the name for the time when your body starts to change from child to young adult. These changes happen over several years and at different rates for different people. It's a time that every adult remembers and although it can have the highs, lows, twists and turns of a rollercoaster ride, it can be amazing too!

You might feel excited, curious or a bit overwhelmed. Knowing what to expect will help you feel more in control.

GIRL TO GIRL

"I'm worried because I've been going through puberty for two years now. But I don't seem to be growing breasts. Perhaps they'll never grow!"

"I used to be a tomboy, but now I'm going through puberty and all of a sudden I like more girly stuff. I feel awkward near boys. I'm scared about it because I don't want to change too much."

"Since I started my periods I often feel confused and like I'm in a weird dream. I forget things and I worry a lot about the meaning of life. My mom thinks it's just because I'm growing up. Does anyone else feel like this?"

Puberty doesn't mean you have to grow up completely!

Diary

What's going on?

Stories from my life

Hey world!

It's Sophie's party on Saturday and it's going to be AWESOME. She's hiring a DJ, there's going to be a barbecue and – most exciting thing ever – her brother Harry is going to be there with his friends.

He's 15 and shy and totally cute. He has this floppy hair and when I think about it I get butterflies in my tummy. It's funny; I've known him for ages, but only recently noticed he was so GORGE!

There's one problem: How do I get him to notice me? I have NOTHING to wear, I blush when I see him and my hair's awful! And, even if he does notice me, he can't get up close, or he'll see all the mega zits on my chin. Gross.

Wait, was that four problems? My life is officially OVER.

A zit? How could this happen?

TOP FIVE... worst party looks

1 *Your new haircut makes you look like a Yeti – but your friend refuses to change the party theme to monster formal!*

2 *You get a huge zit right on the end of your nose. You squeeze it – and make it ten times worse.*

3 *You borrow your best friend's dress. Too late, you realize that her bottom is smaller than yours.*

4 *The body glitter that you thought would make you look cool only succeeds in making your acne sparkle.*

5 *You wear high heels for the first time and trip right over the doorstep!*

GIRL TALK

Real-life advice

If a boy is worth it, he won't care about what you're wearing! But it's understandable that you want to make a good impression. If you're worried about zits, buy some concealer to cover them. Job done!

ARE YOU
normal?

Your body goes through lots of changes during puberty. Here's what's happening.

All change!

Changes to your body and your emotions don't all happen at once. They take place gradually and in a different order for different people.

- **Your emotions start to change.** You experience new sexual feelings.

- **Your periods start.** This usually happens around age 11 or 12, though they may start earlier or later.

- **Your body shape changes.** Your breasts develop, your hips get bigger and you get taller, too.

- **You grow hair.** It seems to suddenly sprout everywhere! Eyebrows, facial hair, pubic hair, underarm hair and hair on your arms and legs.

- **Your vagina produces a clear or creamy discharge.** Your period may be on its way.

- **You may start to get zits.** And you may start to sweat more, too!

Feeling okay?

You could be feeling okay about going through puberty - great! If not, you might be feeling either left behind or scared that things are going too quickly for you. Just because things are happening to you later – or earlier – than your friends, it doesn't mean that there's something wrong. Everyone develops at a different rate.

Everyone's different – even twins!

GiRL TALK

Real-life advice

Puberty can be scary, especially if you hit it before your friends do, but it becomes part of your daily life. In a year or two it will be completely normal – and you won't remember not having breasts or periods!

THE LOWDOWN

When does it happen?

Usually, puberty starts between ages 8 and 13 in girls and 10 to 15 in boys. It ends between the ages of 16 and 19. As girls often go through puberty before boys, don't panic if you suddenly find that you're a lot taller than some of the boys in your class!

YOU AND YOUR breasts

S ome girls look forward to it; others dread it. But when your breasts start to grow, it's hard to hide it! Large breasts get a lot of attention in magazines and on TV, but in the real world, breasts come in all shapes and sizes.

New you!

Your breasts can start to develop from the age of 8 up until 16. Then the breasts start to grow. They may start off pointy but will get rounder.

Breast size is hereditary, which means that there are similarities within your family.

Measuring your breasts every day won't make them any bigger or smaller!

All different

It's easy to worry about the way your breasts develop. Girls with small breasts may think they are unattractive, but girls with large breasts may be teased and can suffer from back pain.

TALKING Point

Bras didn't exist until the later part of the 19th century. What do you think women in the past wore under their clothes?

All about you — Choosing a bra

As your breasts develop, it's important to wear a good bra to support them. A good way to do this is to get yourself measured. Many department stores provide this service.

The best person to go shopping with is your mom or a female relative. Just be direct with her: Ask, "Can you help me go shopping for a bra?" and take it from there.

If your breasts are not big enough for a bra, but you feel uncomfortable about not covering up, a crop top or sports bra can be a good alternative.

PERIODS CAN BE A
pain!

Many girls are excited about starting their periods, but they are probably less happy about going through aches and pains every month. Different girls feel different amounts of pain, and some have no pain at all.

Periods don't have to be a problem if you are prepared!

Diary date

It's a good idea to keep a note in your diary of when your periods start and finish to make sure you are prepared. Don't panic if they are not regular – it may take time for them to settle into a pattern.

Period pain

If you suffer from period pain, here are some things that can relieve it:

* **Mild exercise.** Try stretching, yoga or a short walk.

* **A warm bath or shower.** Or, apply a hot water bottle or heating pad to the area. Make sure you wrap the hot water bottle so as not to burn your skin.

* **Painkillers.** Medication such as ibuprofen will help with very bad cramps.

* **Get help.** Speak to your doctor if the pain seems unbearable.

> *Hands up if you've started your periods! Um... Brian, did you hear the question?*

Keeping it real:
Emergency kit

- ☑ Clean pair of underwear
- ☑ Two or three pads (or tampons if you are comfortable using them)
- ☑ A small packet of wet wipes
- ☑ Money – in case you need to buy more pads from a dispenser
- ☑ Disposal bags – in case there's no bin in the toilet stall

If you find yourself stuck at school with no pads, go to the school nurse's office and they will help. Some girls keep a change of pants and underwear in their locker – or a long sweatshirt to wear or tie around their waist in case of accidents!

EMBARRASSING bodies

It's not just periods. Puberty hormones have a lot of other things to answer for! During puberty, they make your hair and skin more oily, you sweat more (and it smells worse) and you are likely to get zits. Great...

Sweat? Me? I never sweat!

Body smells

Teen sweat is different from kid sweat. It smells more – and nobody likes the smell of BO (that stands for body odor!) Luckily, it's not hard to keep it under control. Buy a deodorant and use it. Take a shower and change your clothes every morning. Not sure if you smell? Ask someone you trust to tell you the truth— it will be worth it.

THE LOWDOWN

Zits and what to do about them

Zits are a fact of life when you're a teenager, although some people have it much worse than others. The most common areas for zits are faces, shoulders and backs. There are lots of anti-acne face washes and creams on the market. Ask a pharmacist for help if you don't know what to choose. If your skin is very bad, your doctor can prescribe something.

Some people say that zits can be made worse by eating the wrong food, or not washing enough. Don't believe them – these are myths! Meanwhile, here's a list of what really can make your zits worse.

✳ **Squeezing and picking.** Doing this can drive the zit deeper into the skin, can sometimes spread infection and can even cause scarring.

✳ **Stress.** This can aggravate zits, so try to manage your stress levels.

✳ **Oily makeup or moisturizer.** Look for products labelled "noncomedogenic," as these won't clog pores.

✳ **Menstruation.** During your period, hormonal changes can make zits worse. A good skin care routine may help.

Zits? Yes. But a cute smile, too.

Eighty percent of teens suffer from zits to some degree.

BAD HAIR days!

Have you ever woken up and found that nothing works for your hair, no matter what you do? It happens to everyone – and it can color your mood for the rest of the day. Like the rest of the body, your hair changes at puberty, often becoming greasier and harder to manage. So, what can you do to help?

Bad hair solutions

✳ **Get a great haircut.** This will help prevent bad hair days from happening. Ask your hairdresser for a low-maintenance style that suits your face shape.

✳ **Pick a product.** Use the right shampoo and conditioner. If your hair is too frizzy, dry or oily, there is a formula for you.

✳ **Wash your hair regularly.** Only shampoo your hair once, not twice, and try not to massage your scalp too hard. Always rinse away all traces of conditioner before you leave the shower.

Split ends – or the end of the world?

THE LOWDOWN

What is a "bad hair day" anyway?

A "bad hair day" is when you wake up feeling really negative about yourself. You look in the mirror and suddenly your tried-and-true favorite outfit looks weird, your face looks wrong and, well, you just don't want to leave the house!

I knew it was going to be a bad day when my favorite hairbrush turned on me!

If you find yourself having a day when nothing seems right, focus on the fact that you are more than just your hair or your looks. Start by forgiving yourself for not being perfect (who is?), and then try to work towards a more positive attitude. You are important and no one should be allowed to put you down – especially not you!

Quiz

PUBERTY matters!

How much do you know about puberty? Answer true or false to the questions below, and then find out your score!

I've been studying for hours, and I still don't know when my period's due.

1. Puberty can start as early as age 8 in girls.

True/False

2. Other people can always tell if you have your period.

True/False

3. During puberty, girls grow more hair on their arms and legs.

True/False

4. Hair around your vagina is called public hair.

True/False

5. BO stands for body odor.

True/False

6. Eating sweets causes acne.

True/False

7. A heating pad can help with stomach cramps.

True/False

8. Breast buds are a type of exotic flower.

True/False

9. You can't wear a tampon if you are a virgin.

True/False

10. Acne is a very common skin disease.

True/False

HOW MANY DID YOU GET RIGHT?

1-4

Mmm... maybe you should go back over the last few pages again. It's good to know what's going on with your body.

5-7

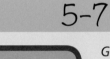

Good job! You still have a bit to learn about puberty, but don't panic! You're in the right place.

8-10

Awesome! You are totally clued in on the subject of puberty. Ever thought about writing a book?

ANSWERS

1. True	6. False
2. False	7. True
3. True	8. False
4. False	9. False
5. True	10. True

Making the most of you!

Stories from my life

Two days to go to the party and Mom said we could go shopping for a new dress. I said I'd rather have jeans and one of those stretchy tops from my magazine. I showed her the picture and she said no way was I wearing anything that tight and I already had enough pairs of jeans.

So, I went over to Sophie's house to see if she had any clothes I could borrow. I took a look through her stuff but, seriously – no way am I going to wear any of it. To put it politely, we just don't have the same kind of style. So I said thanks, but no thanks. I think she was a bit annoyed with me.

I could hear Harry talking to his friends on the phone in the room next door, but I made sure he didn't see me. Why? I've used medicated face scrub on my zits, and it has made my face a bit itchy and red. Not a good look. I am in DESPAIR.

Fashion rule: Just because she looks good in it, doesn't mean you will.

TOP FIVE... ways to deal with stress!

1. Talk to someone you trust about what is making you feel stressed out.

2. Exercise. Go for a swim or try a dance class.

3. Find somewhere you can be on your own to clear your head.

4. Do something you really enjoy to take your mind off the problem.

5. Listen to your favorite music.

DON'T WORRY!

GIRL TALK

Real-life advice

When you're at a party, just enjoy it. Once you're there, it won't matter what you're wearing! If you need a simple way to brighten up your outfit, just add accessories like a nice scarf or bracelets.

confidence

I hate my skinny legs!

I wish I were taller!

Look in the mirror and what do you see? A gorgeous you looking right back? Or are you more critical about your own image? Don't worry: some things you can fix, and the rest you can learn to love!

Be beautiful— in your own way!

If you are down on yourself because of the way you look, remember that all people – even film stars and supermodels – dislike some part of their bodies.

We all have to live with the face shape, height and build we were born with. So make the most of your best features. If you're tall, don't slouch to make yourself look shorter. If you're shapely, enjoy your curves. There is nothing more attractive than confidence!

Nobody is 100 percent happy with her looks. Even the prettiest girl in your class will have parts of her body she doesn't like.

THE LOWDOWN

"Real" girls vs. models

When you open a fashion magazine, you're confronted with pages of "perfect" people—women who are slim, pretty and wearing clothes to die for. The truth is that real girls don't look like that. Models and celebrities are styled before photo shoots and social events. They have

professionals to do their makeup, hair and clothes. Then fashion editors choose the very best images of them. The images are often digitally manipulated to remove zits and quirky parts.

It's great to look at fashion mags and get inspiration for your look, but don't compare yourself to models or celebrities. In fact, have you seen an image of a celeb with no makeup? That's right – she's not so perfect after all!

It's easy for a computer to smooth away imperfections.

True beauty comes in all shapes and sizes!

TALKING *Point*

Why don't fashion magazines use models of all different shapes and sizes? What do YOU think?

WHAT'S YOUR BODY shape?

Are you an apple?

As you grow and develop, your body shape changes. In fact, between the ages of 11 and 16, your height alone will have changed by up to 12 inches (30.5 cm). By around the age of 16, you will have your adult body!

One subject crops up in magazines a lot, and that's body shape. Four shapes that you might read about are ruler, hourglass, apple, and pear – often with advice about what fashions best suit these shapes. It's easy to read these sorts of articles and end up judging yourself. Of course, it's a good idea to wear clothes that suit you, but don't overthink it. Remember, you're probably still growing and your shape is changing.

RULER
Your shape is straight up and down.

HOURGLASS
You have a narrow waist and your top and bottom halves balance.

APPLE
Your whole shape is rounded.

PEAR
Your bottom half is wider than your top half.

The best advice is not to get too obsessed with categories. It's likely that your body doesn't fit any of them – and that's perfectly fine. Experiment to find out what kind of clothes and accessories show off your best features, no matter what shape you are!

All about you
Fun with fashion!

So you see, I think that belt would look much better on me.

I bet an apple would look awful in this hat!

The best way to find out what suits you is to try on things. Sometimes outfits that look terrible on the rack turn out to be great when you're wearing them, so don't be afraid to try something different.

Take a friend with you who will tell you the truth. And if she tries on something that you think is SO wrong, you're allowed to tell her – nicely!

GIRL TALK

Real-life advice

There's never any point worrying about your body shape, because everyone wants what they don't have! No two bodies are the same, but that's what makes you unique.

Dressing

FOR YOU!

Fashion is a form of self-expression, right? So why do most people follow the same trends and end up all looking the same?

Fashion: the facts

When you are a teen, there's a lot of pressure to dress the "right" way. One of the reasons for this is that people like to belong to a group, and following fashions makes you feel included.

However, some people use fashion to make themselves stand out from the crowd. They wear something different to say "Hey, look at me – I'm an individual!"

Whatever your approach, don't feel like you HAVE to wear the latest thing just because everyone else does. Even if purple is the hottest color, there's no need to dye your hair purple, even if your best friend does. Save it for your nail polish!

Did I go too far with the purple?

TOP FIVE... fashion face-offs with your parents!

1. **Bending the rules.** Your parents want you to do well at school and not irk teachers by breaking the dress code. It's best to keep your more extreme fashion for out of school!

2. **Short skirts.** Your parents might find it hard to see their girl growing up and dressing in a way that is attractive to boys. You could offer to tone down your look when you're visiting relatives.

3. **High heels.** Go shoe shopping with your mom and come to a compromise for everyday wear. Then she might get you some different shoes for party wear!

4. **Makeup.** Young skin often doesn't need a lot of makeup, but if makeup is your thing, keep it to a minimom for school.

5. **Piercings and tattoos.** In most cases, you need parental consent to get these done if you are under 18. Check the law and talk to your parents first!

THE LOWDOWN

Quick fact

In the United States alone, $250 billion is spent on fashion EVERY single year!

BEAUTY routine

Great skin goes a long way in helping you look good! Here's what you need to know about your skin and how to keep it in tip-top condition.

OMG! What's that on my chin?

Don't panic! Most people get zits at some point between the ages of 11 and 20. Zits are caused by changes in hormone levels during puberty, when the skin produces excessive amounts of an oily substance called sebum. Sebum is the bad guy: it blocks the pores in the skin and causes blackheads and whiteheads. Occasionally these become infected and get filled with pus. Yep, that means acne!

Mirror, mirror, in my place, what's this zit doing on my face?

Keeping it real:
Get the radiant look!

 Cleanse your skin. Use a mild soap or cleanser every morning and at night before you go to bed. And DON'T go to bed with makeup on!

Moisturize. Protect your face with a light moisturizer. Choose one with a UV sunscreen to protect yourself from the sun.

 Brighten your complexion. Exfoliate once a week. This means rubbing away dead skin cells from the top layer of your skin. You can use a damp washcloth for mild exfoliation or you can buy exfoliating scrub creams.

If you've got zits: Go to your pharmacy or doctor if zits are causing you a problem or making you feel unhappy. There are plenty of treatments to try, so don't suffer in silence.

Don't forget! Drink plenty of water and get enough sleep. You need at least eight or nine hours a night.

> Never squeeze your zits! It will only make them worse.

THE LOWDOWN

Beware the sun!

Sun damage can happen any time you're out in sunny weather. Always protect yourself: use UV sunscreen on exposed skin and wear a hat if it's really hot.

DO YOU HAVE BODY
confidence?

How confident are YOU about your own body? Answer the questions and follow the arrows to find out!

START HERE!

Do you smile when you talk to people you don't know?
- NO
- YES

When you buy clothes, do you always stick to styles you know best?
- YES
- NO

Do you look down when you walk?
- YES
- NO

Are you always up for trying the latest hairstyle – even if it is a bit far-out?
- NO
- YES

When someone pays you a compliment, do you always believe them?
- NO
- YES

Everybody wants to know where I got my new dress!

Do you often think that clothes look awful on you?

YES

NO

CONFIDENCE CRISIS

Oh dear, you're not feeling very confident right now, but try not to worry. Everyone is beautiful in her own way – including YOU!

Do your friends sometimes come to you for fashion advice?

NO

YES

CONFIDENCE BOOST

You're mostly confident but sometimes have doubts. Give yourself a boost: think about all your good features!

Do you pretty much always like what you see in the mirror?

NO

YES

CONFIDENCE QUEEN

You've got the knack of feeling – and looking – confident about your body. That's great, so don't change that!

Would you pose for your school's photography class?

NO

YES

Looking good!

Stories from my life

I nearly didn't go the party. Then Mom had a chat with me at breakfast. She said sorry we'd had a fight, and I said sorry too. Then we went shopping! She bought me a new pair of jeans, and I used my allowance to get some awesome colored braids to put in my hair. No more bad hair days for me!

I stopped using that face scrub and my skin calmed down a bit. In fact, the zits are almost gone – with some help from a bit of concealer, that is.

And, the party was so much fun. I didn't talk to Harry until right at the end, when the DJ was playing some slow, smoochy songs. Then he came over, and he only asked me to dance with him! OMG, I nearly died. We danced right up until it was time to go home. No kissing – but that's fine. You never know what's going to happen in the future, right?

Life is looking up.

Best. Party. Ever!

GIRL TO GIRL

"Sometimes, I look in the mirror and don't like what I see. Then I realize that I am frowning or looking worried. I put on a big smile and look again – and I always look a lot better!"

"I think that becoming a teen is like moving from one world (child) to another (adult). You lose confidence because you go from somewhere where you have learned the rules to somewhere where you need to learn them again. It can take time before you feel OK about yourself again."

"I was feeling really insecure about my looks and unsure about how to wear makeup the right way. So I went to one of the makeup counters at a department store. They did a free consultation and showed me how to apply makeup in the best way for my coloring. It was a great boost!"

THE LOWDOWN

Quick fact!

Psychologists have found that when you're feeling down, you can actually lift your mood by making yourself smile!

STAY IN shape!

You've only got one body, so it's best to take care of it! Here are some top tips for staying healthy, fit and fabulous.

Exercise – are you getting it?

You need exercise to stay in shape. It keeps your heart healthy and strengthens your bones and muscles. You need at least one hour a day of exercise that makes your heart beat faster. This could be as simple as going for a quick walk or an easy bike ride. Then three times a week you need to push it a bit harder, for example, with dancing, swimming or a tougher bike ride.

Exercise doesn't have to be difficult. Walking the dog, dancing, skateboarding— it all counts!

TOP FIVE...
tips for eating well

1   *Eat a balanced diet to get all the nutrients you need.*

2   *Eat five portions of fruits and vegetables a day. A portion is about a handful. (Good news: one portion can be a glass of juice. Bad news: potatoes don't count!)*

3   *Don't skip breakfast. Breakfast wakes up your body and gets you ready for the day's action.*

4   *Teenage girls often lack iron in their diet, so if you don't eat much meat (or if you're a vegetarian) have iron-rich snacks, such as raisins, apricots or unsalted nuts.*

5   *Make sure that you have plenty to drink. Water is best, as it contains no sugars to damage your teeth, but milk is also good. Keep carbonated, caffeinated or sugary drinks to a minimum.*

IT'S OK TO BE different

It's easy to compare ourselves to other people, and feel self-conscious about being different. You might wish sometimes that you were more like everyone else. But it's our differences that make us who we are!

Why me?

It's normal to feel uncomfortable sometimes about the things that make you stand out from others. Maybe you have worse acne than your friends or hate having to wear braces. Whatever the reason, if you feel self-conscious about the way you look, you might find yourself saying, "Why me?"

If your feelings are affecting your relationships with your friends, then try talking to them about it. You could also find a friendly adult to help. If you can't speak easily to your parents, try a teacher or health adviser.

Braces aren't so bad. My friend has them too – and we know our teeth are going to look awesome when the braces come off!

GIRL TO GIRL

"People teased me about my new glasses and I hated wearing them. Then I decided glasses are cool, and now I don't even think about them—or the people who teased me!"

"When I moved to a new school, I could tell that my classfriends were finding it hard to see past the wheelchair. But once they got to know me, they treated me the same as anyone else. And if someone didn't, that was their problem."

"I'm taller than the rest of the girls in my grade. For a while I felt like everyone was judging me, and I felt pretty miserable about it. But recently I discovered that several friends are actually jealous of my height."

TALKING *Point*

Have you ever felt horribly self-conscious about the way you look? How did you get over it?

HOW HEALTHY IS
your lifestyle?

Now that you know what it takes to stay fit and healthy, put yourself to the test! Answer the questions and jot down your answers. See which letter you picked the most. Then check out your results.

I'm updating my status about what I had for breakfast. The world needs to know!

1 How many portions of fruits and vegetables do you eat a day?
   a *One*
   b *Three*
   c *Five*

2 How many times a week do you exercise and break a sweat?
   a *Once*
   b *Twice*
   c *Three times*

3 In sunny weather, when do you use UV sunscreen?
   a *When I notice my skin burning*
   b *When I remember*
   c *Every time I go out in the sun*

4 How much water do you drink every day?
   a *I don't drink much water.*
   b *One or two cups*
   c *At least five cups*

5 How much sleep do you get most nights?
   a *Six hours or less*
   b *Seven hours*
   c *At least eight hours*

6 How many times a day do you drink carbonated drinks?
   a *Two or three times*
   b *Once*
   c *Never*

7 How often do you skip breakfast?
   a *Every day*
   b *Only if I'm running late.*
   c *Never*

8 What's your favorite after-school snack?
   a *Sweets*
   b *Toast*
   c *Fresh fruit*

Mostly As

Hmm... you need to pick up a few more healthy habits. You'll soon look and feel much better!

Mostly Bs

You're doing okay, but there are some things you could improve on. Did you get enough sleep last night?

Mostly Cs

Hey, your healthy lifestyle is right on track. Keep on riding your bike and eating those healthy snacks!

Boy talk

FROM HIS POINT OF VIEW

He may have mood swings and feel emotional.

He may get zits.

His voice begins to break. Just for a while, he may sound croaky or have a high voice one moment and a low voice the next.

He grows pubic hair and hair on his legs, arms, face, chest and armpits.

He gets taller and more muscular.

For a guy, there isn't just one sign that he is growing up; there are lots. And, like a girl, he can feel confused, too!

His larynx (or voice box) grows and sticks out in the front. This is called the Adam's apple.

Growing up

Most boys begin puberty between the ages of 9 and 14, but like girls, all boys grow at their own pace. And – like girls – boys are very aware of the changes that are taking place. They often think they are starting puberty too late or worry that what is happening to them is not happening to anyone else!

All these things are happening to HIM during puberty.

○ BOYS SAY...

"I often wonder whether what's happening to me is normal, but you can't talk to other guys about this stuff. My parents don't want to talk either. Sometimes I get worried, but it's easy to be lazy and do nothing about it."

"I don't know why, but every time I shut my eyes I think of girls. I'm 14 and I know I'm going through puberty, so I guess this is normal? I think about girls that I see on the bus or in the street. Sometimes I smile at them, but they don't seem to notice me."

"It may sound silly, but I'm worried about my height. My friends have had lots of growth spurts and some are over 6 feet (182 cm) tall! I don't want to be the shortest guy in the class."

HEALTHY you!

I f you look after your health, you're likely to have higher energy levels, perform better at school and feel happier, too. And there are two important things that will give your health a boost — eating and sleeping well.

Yay! Healthy people feel more positive.

A weighty issue

Many girls worry about being overweight. However, being too thin is just as dangerous to your health as being too heavy. For that reason, it's important to think about eating well — having a healthy diet, rather than being ON a diet. Everyone has her own normal weight range, depending on lots of factors. If your best friend is thinner than you, that doesn't mean you're overweight!

If you eat the right amount of healthy foods and you get enough exercise, the chances are that your weight is fine. If you're in any doubt about your weight, ask your parents or check with a school nurse.

Keeping it real:
Sleep routine

☑ **Get enough sleep.** You need eight or nine hours sleep on a school night. Nobody wants to go to bed early, but according to scientists, you'll be smarter if you get some shut-eye.

☑ **Get a routine.** Go to bed and get up at the same time every day. Your body likes routines.

☑ **Get comfortable.** Make sure your bedroom is cool, quiet and relaxing. If you're sleeping on a lumpy old pillow, get a new one!

☑ **Stop worrying.** If you're losing sleep because of a problem, talk it over with someone. Sharing will lighten the load—and help you sleep.

☒ **Don't overindulge.** Don't eat too much or drink caffeinated drinks (tea, coffee or cola) before bedtime. It will keep you awake.

TALKING *Point*

How healthy is your lifestyle? What one thing could you do today to make your lifestyle healthier?

FAQs

You can look for advice about puberty online, but don't believe everything people tell you in the chat rooms.

Q **What makes puberty start?**

A *Your body knows when it wants to start, and you can't hurry it up or slow it down. When the time is right, and your body and mind are ready, your brain sends a signal to your ovaries for puberty to begin.*

Q **I really don't want to go through puberty. I'm just too scared. What can I do?**

A *Remember that you're not alone. All adults went through this and so will all your friends too. Try to find out more information about puberty: the more you know about the changes that will happen, the better prepared you will be. And the more you understand why and how these changes are taking place, the less scared you will be. Talk to your (trusted) friends who may be feeling the same way. Parents, school counselors, school nurses and doctors can all give you advice too.*

Q **Should I see a doctor about my periods?**

A *Talk to your doctor if any of these apply to you:*

- *You are 15 and have not had a period.*
- *Your periods were regular, and now they are not.*
- *Your period comes more often than every 21 days or less often than every 45 days.*
- *Your period lasts more than seven days.*
- *Your periods are so heavy that you have to change your pad or tampon every hour.*
- *Painkillers don't help the cramps.*

 **Is it true that you can lose your virginity with a tampon?**

No, it's not true. You are officially a virgin until you have had penetrative sex. But inserting a tampon may disrupt your hymen, which is a fold of tissue that lines your vaginal opening. Typically your hymen has a hole in it already, which allows your menstrual blood to come out. Many things can disrupt the hymen or cause it to bleed, such as riding a bicycle or a horse, playing other sports and inserting a tampon.

Can a tampon make you ill?

Toxic shock syndrome (TSS) is a rare illness that can lead to death if left untreated. It happens when a cetain type of bacteria gets into the bloodstream. To help avoid this happening, change your tampon regularly and use the correct absorbency for your flow. Look for symptoms such as vomiting, a sudden red rash on the face, dizziness, fever, confusion, muscle aches and diarrhea. If you experience these symptoms when using a tampon, consult a doctor right away.

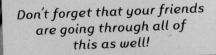
Don't forget that your friends are going through all of this as well!

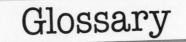

absorbent Good at soaking up liquids.

bad hair day A day when your hair is hard to manage and/or a day when everything seems to go wrong.

body odor (BO) An unpleasant smell that happens when you sweat. This can be helped by washing frequently and using deodorant.

confidence The feeling that you can rely on someone or something. If you have self-confidence, it means that you have belief in yourself.

cramps The sudden, unexpected tightening of muscles. Cramps in the uterus (womb) can cause pain in the abdomen (tummy). This pain can also spread out to the lower back and thighs.

disrupt To break something apart.

genitals Reproductive organs that are on the outside of the body.

hereditary Passed down through a family, from generation to generation.

hormones Chemicals released by cells in the body, which send messages to other cells.

hymen A fold of tissue that partially covers the entrance to the vagina.

mood swing An extreme or very fast change in mood.

ovaries Reproductive organs on the inside of the female body. The ovaries produce eggs, which are released into the womb every month. If an egg is fertilized by a sperm, a baby starts to grow.

periods (menstruation) A woman's monthly bleeding. Every month, the body prepares for pregnancy. If no pregnancy occurs, the uterus sheds its lining, which passes out of the body through the vagina. Periods usually start around age 12 and last from 3 to 5 days.

puberty The physical changes that turn a child's body into an adult body. On average, girls begin puberty at ages 10-11 and complete puberty by 15-17.

pubic hair Hair that grows around the genital area in boys and girls during puberty.

sanitary pad (or napkin) A soft pad that sticks to a woman's underwear during her period and absorbs blood.

stress A physical response to events that make you feel threatened or upset your balance. A little stress is good, as it helps us meet challenges. A lot of stress can damage your quality of life and your health.

symptoms A sign that a disease or condition is present in the body. For example, if you have a cold, the symptoms could be a sore throat or runny nose.

tampon A piece of soft material attached to a string, which is inserted into the vagina during a woman's period to absorb blood.

vagina A passage leading from the uterus to the vulva, part of the female genitals.

Get help!

There are places to go to if you need more help. The following books and Web sites will give you more information and advice.

Further reading

Girls' Guide to Caring for Your Body by Isabel Lluch and Emily Lluch (WS Publishing Group, 2012)

Head-to-Toe Guide to You by Sarah Wassner Flynn (Scholastic, 2010)

Is This Really My Body? Embracing Physical Changes by Holly Saari (ABDO, 2010)

My Beauty: A Guide to Looking & Feeling Great by Marlene Wallach (Aladdin, 2009)

Sexual Health: Understanding Your Body's Changes by Serena Gander-Howser (Rosen Central, 2013)

The Smart Girl's Guide to Growing Up by Anita Ganeri (Scholastic, 2011)

Web sites

Due to the changing nature of Internet links, Rosen Publishing has developed an online list of Web sites related to the subject of this book. This site is updated regularly. Please use this link to access the list:

http://www.rosenlinks.com/GTALK/Zits

Index